The
Haunted Hand

ESSENTIAL TRANSLATIONS SERIES 46

ONTARIO ARTS COUNCIL
CONSEIL DES ARTS DE L'ONTARIO

an Ontario government agency
un organisme du gouvernement de l'Ontario

Canada Council   Conseil des arts
for the Arts   du Canada

Guernica Editions Inc. acknowledges the support
of the Canada Council for the Arts and the Ontario Arts Council.
The Ontario Arts Council is an agency of the Government of Ontario.
We acknowledge the financial support of the Government of Canada through
the National Translation Program for Book Publishing, an initiative
of the *Roadmap for Canada's Official Languages 2013-2018:
Education, Immigration, Communities,* for our translation activities.
We acknowledge the financial support of the Government of Canada.
Nous reconnaissons l'appui financier du gouvernement du Canada.

LOUISE DUPRÉ

The
Haunted Hand

Translated by
Donald Winkler

GUERNICA
EDITIONS

TORONTO · BUFFALO · LANCASTER (U.K.)
2020

Original title: *La main hantée* (2016)
Copyright © 2016, Les Éditions Noroît.
Translation copyright © 2020 Donald Winkler and Guernica Editions Inc.

Michael Mirolla, editor
Cover and interior design: Rafael Chimicatti
Cover image: pedrofigueras | pixabay
Guernica Editions Inc.
287 Templemead Drive, Hamilton (ON), Canada L8W 2W4
2250 Military Road, Tonawanda, N.Y. 14150-6000 U.S.A.
www.guernicaeditions.com

Distributors:
Independent Publishers Group (IPG)
600 North Pulaski Road, Chicago IL 60624
University of Toronto Press Distribution,
5201 Dufferin Street, Toronto (ON), Canada M3H 5T8
Gazelle Book Services, White Cross Mills
High Town, Lancaster LA1 4XS U.K.

First edition.
Printed in Canada.

Legal Deposit—First Quarter
Library of Congress Catalog Card Number: 2019947051
Library and Archives Canada Cataloguing in Publication
Title: The haunted hand / Louise Dupré ; translated by Donald Winkler.
Other titles: Main hantée. English
Names: Dupré, Louise, 1949- author. | Winkler, Donald, translator.
Series: Essential translations series ; 46.
Description: Series statement: Essential translations series ; 46 |
Translation of: La main hantée.
| Poems.
Identifiers: Canadiana 20190156902 | ISBN 9781771835107 (softcover)
Classification: LCC PS8557.U66 M3413 2020 | DDC C841/.54—dc23

1

*It's as hard for a fly to die
as it is for the most powerful lord.*

—EDMOND JABÈS

No one ever taught you
to fashion yourself
a shell

to ward off nightmares
that dwell

in the tenuous silence
of your sheets

all night you dreamed
of soldiers marching
to the pulse of fanfares

to the delight of passers-by
always ready to revel

each night has its pageant
its war
set to music

pitched down on cries
the ghosts
of executions

in the morning you awoke
from shame

to at once turn back
to shame

you fondled your cat
you imprisoned it
in its cage

and under the indifferent sun
you came with it

to this still empty
room

where you wait
your muscles numbed

as if it were you
the condemned

it howls, your cat
and you can no longer bear
to hear it

gasping for breath
its despair so humble

that you don't know
how to name

the entreaties, the appeals
of a creature
wanting to save its life

you do not know by what right
you've determined
its end

by what right
you take yourself for God

you want to flee
the cage welded
to your hand

but you stay put
rooted to the howling
in your ear

while the receptionist
before you
toils away

mindless
of your distress

he looks at you, your cat
his eyes already dead

unable to fathom
your cruelty

and you beg
his forgiveness

you ask forgiveness
for all who will die
today

humans
or tongue-tied animals

life's outcasts
worn to the bone

but beasts don't kill themselves
even in unspeakable
pain

they wait to be swathed
in darkness

perhaps he would have wanted
to go on suffering
your cat

like all those felines
from the dawn of time

but you propel him
towards a modern
death

when he was only asking
for his daily meal

ideas, images
and words blur
the stillness of the room

and you try to enter
the minds of executioners

just before they slip
the stool from under the feet
of the hanged

or plunge a needle
into the artery
of a murderer

but you're alone here
with these more and more unendurable
yowls

you choose
to allot the task
to a woman

paid to administer
what she calls
the protocol

she asks you to follow her
and you follow, your eyes
empty

and the cat
suddenly mute from fear

you barely hear
the word *sedative*

you open the cage
door

you clutch the animal
close

and let the woman
plant a needle
in his skin

thinking of this loved one
nearing his end

so tiny
so old
that he can hope for no more

love is love
and you could still
spare him

but you are impassive
your cat enfolded
in your voice

which dwindles away
beneath sing-song phrases

as for a child
you're putting to sleep

after its day's
last milk

he no longer howls
your cat

now consoled
by your hands'
scent

hands that caressed him so often
fed him and caressed him

and brushed him each night
in front of the television
news

black silk, rich silk
so hot sometimes
in hours of illness

that you fretted
about pain and its ways

with the living
below the threshold of words

how to impart care
when nothing is certain

how to convey
the goodwill

of the small tortures
we call *treatments*

you turn in circles
with your questions

watching the minutes
press on
too fast on the clock

the woman in white
returns
with the dead

and you lower to the table
what has fled already

you mouth
a mother's mute words

you touch the cheek
thinking of the condemned

done in
by hate

and you begin to cry
when the little heart
stops

you weep
as you've not wept
for a long time

and you continue to stroke
the tepid remains

talking
as we talk to the dead

but one must return
to life
and light

the cage suspended
from the end of your arm

and the heart
forgone

the heart now
split off

as in a canvas
of Frida Kahlo

and you see again
the last tableau

as you store away
the round basket
the toys and the brush

feeling as if you're killing
your cat
once more

you'll be left only
with pictures

folded over all that's shaming
in a sadness

where there echoes
the howling of all
black cats

burned alive
in the age of witchcraft

you'd like to open your arms
to the pyres
gone back to dust

and in a language common to all
you dig

the same grave
for beasts and women

possessed by the devil
of superstition

there you are beak and claws

as always
when an ancient memory comes forth

your pain dormant
deep
in your breast

and you, consoled

by the picture of your cat
at peace
in a death

you would wish for yourself
when you too
will be blind and deaf

a little injection
and you will snuff out

like a flame
at the end of hope

and you will go to rejoin
the band
of vertebrates

slumbering in the hereafter
of their ashes

but your sin

that wound
you cleanse too readily
with your clear conscience

you had him
vanish
without his consent, your cat

like a daughter
her mother

when she refuses
a life stubbornly
prolonged

suddenly you can no longer
tell good
from evil

nor purgatory from hell
where you find yourself

among guilty
souls

it is there within you
this blaze
of suffering

there the howls
that return
to disturb your solitude

all those animals
hurled alive
onto the trash heap

dead from hunger
at the ends of their chains

or beaten
until they die

and you weep with Nietzsche
before this old horse
lashed by the whip

for philosophy is impotent
in the face of the malice
of masters

to wash away pain
there are only tears

and poetry when it comes
to touch
the marrow of language

alone now
with your hand

you blacken pages
and pages

since you need a place
to lodge the shame

that could end
by killing you

as you yourself
killed your cat

when all he begged for
was a reprieve

you remained deaf
as a stone

you, reputedly
merciful

blessed among
women

now are you banished
from the great garden

you wander
in search
of redemption

you now know murder
clings to your skin

like a tick
resolved to suck
the last of your blood

you belong to a race
domesticated
in the shadow of churches

but you still speak
as do we all

a language
barbaric

And we hear the distant echo
Of this call, an awful noise –
A lapping, a predator's cry, a complaint,
And before us a vision: crossed hands.

—ANNA AKHMATOVA

You can kill even someone you love, we sometimes decide to kill what we love. It has wormed its way bit by bit into your brain, it howled, your cat, it never stopped howling, and you no longer wanted to hear. You could bear it no more, like the mother who could no longer bear to hear her child cry. All it took was to press a pillow over the little mouth, and then no more. The child went quiet. You, you dialled a telephone number, you happened on a woman's voice and you answered her *Yes*. And yet it would never enter your mind to write *I am guilty*. You would then be one with your remorse.

The howls of starving babies, the howls of women giving birth, the howls of prisoners being tortured, the silent howls of wives stoned to death, of girls and boys being raped, howls of rapists, of murderers, the last howls of assassins that nobody hears, howls of the deported, the bombarded, the lambs their throats slit, howls of slaves deep in holds, of witches at the stake, of warriors, of the dying at the far point of their suffering, howls of appeal, of revolt, of despair, the howls of your cat. Howls you never answered to.

You hear the howls choked back in the earth's entrails each time you set your feet on the ground, you would hear them even if you were to kill all that is alive. You ask each time to be delivered from evil, but who could reach out a hand to you, what word would free you from despair? You belong to a line so long that it no longer remembers on what continent it was born, fish, birds, carnivores, mammals that little by little stood upright and learned to walk, a race of hunters, pillagers, criminals. On your hands the millenary smell of fire and blood.

You come from a throng of women sold off, fattened for the glory of the species, you come from survival. You are a skein of tangled threads, *the victim and the oppressor*, nighttime's despair, the woman whose sleep is haunted by generations that learned the strength and submission of words, you remember it whenever you waken within yourself the ancient dead. You go back then to the inscrutable signs on stone, to the gravity of shadows that depict the souls of beasts. You return to your humble insect body, spider of the shades, giant mother, unmoving, who hovers over her eggs before a museum. Your work with flesh and new beginnings.

The word *goodness*, it brings back your childhood vernacular, noon bells, the school, you've squirreled it all away deep in old closets. The sky's four corners are lit up now like fireworks, bombs, rockets, the chemistry of war, the world veers every day from one death throe to another, and you must each day zap the adversity before it sets your eyes on fire. You seek to hold your head high even if you can only swallow what's sullied, like the crusts of bread birds beg for. You too beg, for a bit of warmth, a ray of light, you do not want to add to the desolation. Because you know, despite the eruption of images, the soul has not changed since the division of waters and dry land.

You are like all those mothers who have always protected their children, fed them, licked them, taught them, devoured them in front of predators. You would like to revive your line of hairy ancestors, you, born with a body so naked you can trace with your finger the blue paths of your veins. You are a thin-skinned geography, and you think of the great migrations of those before you who didn't know how to talk, of their bellowing in your sleep, bellowing that rips at the sky when words gutter out in your mouth. You then understand the arrogance of your language, and its poverty. How to write *I* if you don't believe in the human race?

How to write when suffering as an animal suffers? You hark back to the rough-hewn furry languages, you would like to talk dog or cat, to know what is felt when a woman shuts the cage that will convey us to our eternity, you would like to know if, on the last morning, the breeze takes on the scent of leaves or ashes. You would like to undo the distress in nanoseconds, swallow it, imprison it in your bones, that it welcome the shadow of the poem like a second chance, a fearful trembling within you, an abject soul you would learn to approach without contempt. You could then write *I*, as if this pronoun at last opened out, became a cavern, a porous stone you'd need only caress with the palm of your hand for fossil forms to issue forth from forgetfulness.

You began this book without asking yourself why, and since, you have sought no response. You are content with this image, a blot on your hand, as in a Rorschach test. Your poems foresee no radiance or grace, they break down always in the backwash of words, they make their way over shipwrecks and blood spat down upon the page. It's a small thing, to write, a babbling that would like to be confession, but you would have to place yourself then at the core of the morning, wipe away its dew, its quotidian tears. You write small so that the language, if you approach it without conceit, will no longer conceal its impotence. You will never have said all, you will be someone else forever, the girl spurned by the heavens, impaled upon her cruelty.

You forged for yourself, over time, an entire arsenal, clubs, large crosses, knives, steel idioms you learned to bury in the tenderest flesh. Words do not bloody the hands, they are your best weapon, and you can continue in peace to put one foot in front of the other in accord with law and order, to roam abroad haloed in innocence. But the night surprises you in the end, and you hear the tumult in your soul, too great a burden to be hidden behind good intentions. You see again your old cat, you see again all your crimes and all the animals, those you gave away, drowned, killed, in a life you no longer want to see as your own.

There you are again in an inferno of images dancing in the flames. Night brings you no consolation, only a question looping about your tongue, *What have you done forever and ever?* You seek a blessing, a repose you do not deserve. You would perhaps have to light a candle and see the glow scale the wall of your room to imagine that you might once more sleep in peace. But no one will come to tuck you in, no one will be there to remove the stain from your hand, you will be prey to sorrow right to the end. Because you are not free from blame, you begin now to see it. Now you glimpse the day when you will confess it. When you will be strong enough to write *I*.

2

I am the cry and the wound,
I am the woman at your side
who is maligned and defiled.

—ANNE HÉBERT

No one ever taught you
to take down

the little corpses
the girls
swinging from ropes in trees

like kites
soiled
by urban sperm

they are there this morning
in their Indian robes

before your half-open
eyes

they parade
like cats
seeking a home

and the Facebook fury
of women
like you

undone
by each jolt
of their computer

you would never have been able
to imagine

that you could be raped
and hanged

on the way to urinate
in the fields
by night

never imagined that your eye
would become a gallery
of horrors

where the fates of girls
would be confounded
with those of beasts

and you wonder
how you'll be able to endure
one more day

the heart strafed
by all this suffering

porous
as an old woman

unable to bear
her tears

it wouldn't take much
for despair
to bear you away

one more rape
another child

lying down in blood
amid ruins

a dog
abandoned by a pole
along the highway

like this terrier
found yesterday
by the SPCA

you rise in the morning
your head
filled with darkness

yet it's July
the terraces in flower
and the beaches

but you see only
graves

dug hastily
in cities
of dust

since one has to forestall
epidemics

despite yourself you have become
a tourist of death

and you move on
like a sleepwalker
through the streets

between laughter
and summer jazz

thinking of those
who have not known
how to resist

Marina Tsvetaeva, Sylvia Plath
Huguette Gaulin

and all the unknown ones
asleep for all time
in their pain

but you, you continue
to step across the reported
corpses

holding
to petitions

placed on line
by the despairing

who hope to declare themselves
human

you go on with your life
willing
to believe

the world is stalwart enough
to confront adversity

you do your best to preserve
language
because it has always survived

you want to invent
children who will die
of old age

metaphors
that can disarm
the powerful

proofs more powerful
than the bills

piled up
in banks

you sometimes still
dream of the Earth

as an egg
decorated by a Mother
Courage

you persist in fostering
naïve ideas

when what you see
makes you waver

you compare yourself to a fly
turning about
a candle

with enough watchfulness
to protect itself

what distance must you maintain
between yourself
and the horizon in flames

what love to offer
to the earth's
carbonized face

what love
could save you

you who insist
on living upright

you think of Claude Gauvreau
of Virginia Woolf, of Hubert Aquin

each day you try
to rub
from your lips

the hard wood of words
that laud petrol
and tanks

but no poem
can purge
an entire vocabulary

you have stopped
believing in springs

that can paint cities
red

the soot returns so fast
to soil the maple's
leaves

but you still know how
to resist

and you track down
on your keyboard
an ancestral patience

you want to recall
with enough forgotten
to carry on

you think of Sarah Kane
of Alejandra Pizarnik, of Roland
Giguère

and of those close to you
who you will not name

in these lines that refuse
to succumb

because the poem
is more fragile
than you think

even in July
when you cannot conceive
of a disappearance

but it protects you
from hostile
signs

bringing a little peace
or wisdom

for as long as your journey
lasts

something you crave
as a mercy

while cruelty
goes on with its work

mounting its spectacle
of indifference

and you cling
to the trembling light

seeking words
for goodness

sometimes you say *compassion*
sometimes *pity*

you are prepared
to recycle archaic
synonyms

you are this gleaner
sifting through history

in hopes of unearthing
a few shards

as do beggars
in shameful cities

whom you dare not look
in the eye

or dogs
in indigent lands

you return from each journey
old
with something shrunken

draped
over your shoulders
like a martyrdom

relived
at each crossroads
along your way

you think of Stefan Zweig
of Anne Sexton, of Ernest Hemingway

you ask yourself
who might deliver you
from despair

but your supplications
remain
unanswered

even if you go down
on your knees

you must keep
your eyes
shut tight

to believe
in redemption

you write darkly

you write
with trembling
interrogations

how to pursue
beneath the extinguished
sun

your endless
desert crossing

from whom can you beg
bread and water

when the earth
threatens to swallow you up
at each step

faced with fear
you are but a gaping
hole

where sleeping shadows
stir

between the pages
of the past

for there are books
to remind you
from whence you come

there are those numberless witnesses
to mass graves

and you write with the sadness
of fingers

that exhume
unidentifiable remains

you write "poor"

poor stone
on which you lean

to see it rise
and fall back as quickly

to the foot
of the mountain

you will be Sisyphus
all your life

your sentences
gnawed
by suffering

you think of Nelly Arcan
of Paul Celan, of Seneca
but you write

like a child
each day you do
your duty

you have grown up
bearing upon your palm

the blue scent
of ink

and the alphabet, this miracle
out of time's
silence

it comes to you from far back
to write

as far back
as the human odyssey

and you form your letters
one by one

with the immemorial blood
of hate

as one returns
one's work twenty times
to the loom

you write with an unclean
hand

but you write
the well

which opens
to the light

each time you denounce
the mortification
of a woman

or of a prisoner
being lashed

in petrol's
name

a small gesture, a little
love
set down in the world

like the faded flowers
found
where there were massacres

you, you have only
words to offer

words surfaced
from the shipwrecks' depths

they smell
of rot and urine

but you risk
exposing them
to the sun

in the hope
that they might bring peace
if only to a single soul

you think of Unica Zurn
of Stig Dagerman, of Mayakovsky

of Gérard de Nerval, of Sarah Kofman
of Kawabata

you think of Jean-Pierre Duprey

you are no dupe
to your circle game

but you write

so your blood
will not redden
the world

this you have sworn

we felt guilty
weighed down and guilty
from all the spilled blood encrusted

—ROLAND CIGUÈRE

This you swore. As you would make a vow when you wake in the morning, bug larvae boring into your flesh, a morning so porous it can contain no light. You're emptied out, your mouth empty, dispossessed. You tremble with all the voices that fear all fears, love all loves, despair of all despair. You are no one now, only death throes, a wailing choked back deep within. Back from prehistory you think you are no one, an ancient ape who thought to have escaped unscathed. Nothing and no one, there you are, your breath wed to an agony that is for you too vast. You play dead, you wait for letters to begin stirring once more under your fingers, this you want, you start again to write with this hand suspended, so it may be, at the end of a rope. You will write the word *yes*.

You have no sway over the damnation that dwells within you. You do not move, you would like the silence to spread through the hollow of your ear, the absolution from a silence that would be one with your body, breath with your breath, a war becalmed, a white flag, time enough to take courage, to move on head high into hardship, to remember the vowels in your given name. You want to write *yes*, like Marie, like Molly, like all those who before you answered to love, even deprived of grace you want to write yes, it's enough to wait for your hand to be handed back, nerves and muscles, fingers that dance, do not be afraid, do not be ashamed, play dead until there is fire in the night, until you sear your suffering alive. You will learn then to drink the blood of cities.

Like a sky decomposed, colour of rain, rain of soot, you give yourself over to the angels of darkness body and soul, you belong now to a humanity exiled from blue, and you swim, you exhaust yourself swimming through murky water, not knowing how you will resist. To resist, as in a promise. You think of Virginia, her lost war, her drowned face, you think of all the dead bodies washed up near rivers of tears, you would like to sit them down on your thin knees, warm them, give them your last milk. Then you would bear them to eternal peace. You will judge no more, you will judge yourself no more, you will not be your worst enemy. You could perhaps in time come to forgive yourself.

Your distress has nothing to do with melancholy, nor with the disarray of the poem when it cries with rage, nor with the despair of those who have lost their faith. It is a language with a grammar gone wrong, and the signs begin to wander, to migrate from one phrase to another, something opens inside you, it yawns wide, it brays as on an Easter altar, you are the lamb and the knife of all sacrifices, the expiation and the avenging hand, you are a name split in two, the thought that you might see your last face erased. But there remain to you, luckily, a few metaphors, they shield you from unforgiveable words. You still have a room where you curl up, reciting under your breath the lesson of light.

You learned long ago to evade words that transmit a moribund picture of oceans, that come to hurl themselves against your eyelids, black curtains, raw skin tormenting your sleep. You will always be a refugee from a combat you can never win, that's the way it is, nothing to be done, nothing you can change, you don't know which Lucifer lodged the apocalypse deep in your voice. It's come from so far that you've abandoned your search for this Hades, you only know it echoes like the sound of a knife beneath the throat, the crackling of an oven worn down by cadavers or a child's terror beneath the bombs. It echoes like any comparing that bears within it the music of a lament.

How to regard a poem when it looks you up and down, tries to launch you into the void? You hold to dawn's gaunt silence, you want to believe that your hand can still contain a bit of brightness, just enough to rescue the last word left you. You utter *heart* the way others say *God* or *truth*, it's your only ardour when reason can reason no more, heart, heart beating where a baby sleeps in the arms of its mother, a cat found on a street corner, an ancient voice that suddenly awakens and orders you to rise and walk. And every time you obey, you rise and put one foot in front of another, as if you had never forgotten how to walk. You close the window, leave the world. You accept your treason.

Your terrain was laid out despite you to cover a wound under an open sky, it perturbs the days and their wings, the nights and their wings, where you live there is no repose, there is endless alertness. You would like to deliver all birds from evil, you hang small bells from the necks of cats, and you walk, your head among grey clouds, dreaming that your pitiful gesture might forestall the city's foundering. You will save only a few sparrows, but you act, you dare to act hoping to ease your sorrow a little, since sorrow risks bearing you away. Just a gesture and this word out of another age, *charity*, which you salvage while seeking a way to live, your back to the abyss.

Your back to the abyss, you're a squatter wherever there's a bit of air for survival, it enters your belly with dust from the ground, it gives you stones in your liver, stones in your kidneys, you learn to speak mineral as if you wanted to master the fossils deposited within you, relics of the dead too dead to be reborn in the spring. You bear within you a time that has no more memory of sowing or of grasses maddened by the wind, you are back to the babbling of a world with no lessons to offer, no lands to defend. You might possess all the science of your age, know hundreds of languages, nothing can comfort you. You are a mourning that breaks ceaselessly against the fault of continents, a daily humiliation. You are there, proof perfect that God does not know how to exist.

What would you be if you could escape your fate? A woman with no given name, a soothsayer recruited to read entrails, sacrificial lambs, animals eaten alive by predators, children opened up at knife point. But however you may pilot the future with your naked hands, if will afford you no help. You know the cruelty of cats, you cannot change them and yet you love them. You know people and you love them, perhaps to be awarded a firm dispensation to love yourself. This cowardly odour clings to you like ancient incense, you have often confused it with pain. *Pain*, you have written that word so often that you don't know what meaning to give it. You consent now to hide it in the murmuring of your voice.

And if you transformed yourself, if you became an agent of scorched earth, if you saw yourself as a formless mass, a common grave full to overflowing, one would wonder to what bone you are kin, what destiny, what species threatened or long defunct. You'd have been the link gone missing when called upon, the female with milk-swollen nipples and no other concern than the night to combat and the fire to watch over in the cave. You would consort with pictures so distant that you would no longer despair of your fellows, you would no longer be alone to bear the world's downfall on your shoulders. You would learn to read the present in the imprints of stones, you would no longer be ashamed of seeking consolation.

3

Death will reach me in my left heart
When I have given my blood to time.

—RODNEY SAINT-ÉLOI

No one has ever taught you
to sleep
cheek by jowl with the abyss

there where the ground
emits
the sounds of bones

you would then become
one of the graveyard's
undocumented denizens

the spectre of covert
insults

that demand
reparation

but you no longer dwell
where fables do magic

where predators end
as dogs
worn down from biting

you share a lineage
of scorched wings

a land where the sun falls
in spikes
into the fields

hunger has for a long time doomed you
to kill
with no thought of damnation

and you sport your ferocity
like a reddened
fur

not knowing
from what beast
you have inherited

this stench of flesh
in your nostrils

to what coupling
do you owe this hand

that left
in grottos
its first imprint

you died so often
that you could not tell your age
even if you were begged to do so

you would go back only
to the mouths
of those cannons

now rusted
like spears
out of migrations

your memory's buried face
sleeps

in the tree
where you sheltered
your babies

fearing creatures
more brazen than yourself

you respected then the law
of the jungle

without knowing
those gods

who could sever
heads

with a simple
knife
sharpened for bread

temples, dungeons
windowless schools

firmly grounded
in a syntax
of punishment

you pled guilty
so many times

before bartering
your crown of thorns

for a longing
to deform the sky

as in a new
art

one morning it arrived
swifter than the gloom
on waking

this insight
that teased
your eyelids

and you wished
with all your strength
wished

to heal the love
in you

as if a breeze
could again uplift
your soul

you are not undeserving
of love
you think

and you show yourself ready
to prepare it a nest

since you want
to side
with the living

up against the abyss
it is life
writ small

and its definitions
that you must reinvent
each day

you will never reach the end
of the heart's
lexicon

but you allow yourself
the resolve
to hope

as with these wishes
for the New Year

that you offer
your eyelids half-closed

to mask
the false candour

you say *joy*
and *peace*

skirting thoughts
of children deported

who die
in tents
of cold

or in the hold
of a clandestine boat

you would have good reason
to remain silent

but you renew
the same vows
every year

each year you place your bet
on a card

picked at random
from your superstitions

you keep on
going on

like the poet
of *l'âge*
de la parole

when he made his voice
shimmer

dreaming faces
of a conceivable
tenderness

you keep on
going on

you say *heart*
for *courage*

because now
you know too much

for tears
to wash away
your disgust

the temptation is great
to prefer animals
to your fellows

who show themselves
every day
in a more pitiless light

and so you demand
pity

how to love
the primates
of your species

how to find the courage
to love yourself, you

who are worth no more
than other humans

you caress
your cat
expecting nothing from him

soon he will go and purr
on others' knees

and you will forgive him
as you forgive
an infant

not thinking
he'll become an adult

you want
with all your strength
to see beyond your dreams

a rainbow
of compassion

and at the risk of blinding yourself
you repeat *love*

you say again that your blood
will not redden
the world

you have attained the age
of promises
to keep

and of cloth soft
as cotton
flowers

that you graze
reverently
with your fingernail

remembering the slaves
who sang

beneath the thirst
of a burning sun

you, who never knew
how to make your voice
sing

you are still able
to speak

and you repeat *love*
like *dignity*
or *example*

you need wounds
where you may set your fingers

your faith comes down
to the manifest history
of hurts

inflicted on men
and women
of all longings

history is a pandemic

whose virus
will mutate forever

but you want to go on
planting your pencil

in the arm brandishing
lash
or gun

you will continue to play
the nurse
for incurable causes

as when you were a child
in fights
that you could win

it's so tenuous
carrying on

as intimate
as a journal

whose pages in secret
you blacken

hoping to find
beneath the silence
of words

the welcome you need
to gather up
water from tears

you seek a room
within yourself
open to suffering

wounds to dry
in the morning sun

daisies to set down
in the middle of the table

hospitality, yes
since you consent
to banish yourself

to your own life's
frontier

just a backpack
on your shoulder

you sluff off
your prideful face

to sink down
deep in yourself

to perhaps
soothe
the cry

of the tormented
who will not heal

nor will you heal
that you know

you no longer trust
surgeries
of the soul

you have become over the years
an unbeliever
of whatever faith

and you want
to live
without dogmas

as you write
without dogmas

you have no answer
for suffering

only your ear
to lend

like those books
never
to be returned to you

and here you are at the age
for emptying your bookshelves

you agree
to lose

what you have taken such pains
to gather round you

your future comes down to
this trembling
yes

that you inscribe
on the parchment
of your wrist

so that your blood
will flow on in peace

like an oasis
in the night

when the sky
is pricked
with stars

and you people
your desert
with fraternal voices

that will not betray
your hopefulness

love, you say
is alms

offered
before extending
your hand

a living
draught

you want to offer
in turn

to other thirsting
beggars

it has no commercial value
love

no high or low
season

just an opening
where you see
past your shadow

a tiny
glow

showing you
the way

I teach closed lips
this word strait as death–
love

—Halina Poswiatowska

Where to go when the ground's maw yawns wide beneath your feet? You have seen so many beheadings, so many disembowelled, that you have moved beyond the threshold of shame. You can no longer remain on your knees before the dead, you wrap yourself in a shawl woven from ashes and you hold out your arms to those crying that they are alive. What you call *love* is your escaping yourself a moment to go and pull thorns from the feet of your neighbour. You depart as you would exit a despair too long your home, to go into exile and then return to yourself, fingers dirtied, bloodied, oozing pain and urine, forgoing your image of a woman dead before dying to assume a likeness unlike what was yours. You would then conjure a poetry polished to gleam like a weapon.

You do not remember when the poem turned against you, shook you out like a quilt too accustomed to sleep, forced you to no longer lie. You began to chant unseen melodies for your ear, wrapped in the folds of childhood. They awaited you with the patience of a day ready to dawn, they awaited you, old flesh still bound to bone like faith sprung straight from mire. Music of the street, music of light quivering in the leaves, green music of all the musics that once overhung the earth's complaint. You saw profiled before your eyes beauty's shadow. You who did not concede your debt to pain, you suddenly confess your debt to joy.

It is time to snip the threads between your fingers, to lure stray cats into your garden, to gather up flowers before you are six feet under, to take time enough to bestow grace on dread. You are still human, you still love what you hate, you believe in what you no longer believe, the kindly phantoms of midnight and prayer, even if sullied like a garment that's a familiar of rape. Solitude shouldered, *solitude shattered.* You have not exhausted your nine lives, nor the stars born in your tired eyes, nor the future of simple words. You will find the nerve to lay yourself down like naked snow upon rags in flames, sheer patience countering force and rage, raised up against, upthrust against, white with hope and fear. You will assume control of the field of shame.

No matter if you do not succeed in gauging the true gulf between faith and superstition, you bear the two words like scapulars up against your breasts, like the promise of warm milk. For too long you have provided a haven for the gentle blaze of a dying fall, wooden cross, iron cross, murderous silence of the inferno, and you labour now to think *no* and to patch up your heart, you think *no*, you cry out *no*. You have no more courage than your fellows, only too many suicides within you. You ask their forgiveness and you dig them a grave while telling them the truth, you want to lay down your pain by laying their pain down. So you will be able to hear the bright blood in your veins, the band's music playing on until the foundering of the ship.

You come from a childhood where poets made their end like orphans in asylums, a childhood of blond lambs bleating on allegorical floats, parades without combat, memories crammed into a catechism, images of martyrs ascending to the clouds. They wanted you virginal, missionary, Africa on its knees flowering in churches, they taught you to read the music of sacrifice, and you sang, but off key, your voice breaking like pebbles in the mouths of the drowned. You forgot your animal skin, the hair that plagued you, arms, legs, pubis, weeds you pulled out one by one, you had to play the angel and devoid of talent you played the angel. You began to write, your hand haunted. You are not alone to inhabit your suffering, that you know.

Your hand haunted, you become a story too charged for a woman, one of hair-trigger barbarity. You've known predators of all eras and every era stalks each of your acts. You are a poet of blackened nails and you will remain so. You are no longer of an age for beauty pageants, no longer of an age for verses ringed round in adoration of faces, your mirror replicates now your mother's wrinkles. Aging brings you no peace, no wisdom, only the desolation of a desert where your words can do nothing for hostages cut down by sword blades, like ancient monuments. And yet you dream of poems that will awaken the tenderness of gods, even if you must call them *prayers* or *orisons*. You are your own contradiction.

Prayer, because you have more yet to learn of the evil lodged within you, prayer, love of the earth spread wide like the hips of young girls intent on having the species survive, the future's round belly against all reason, orchards in flower, orchards in fruit, because you must nourish the offspring of women, prayer because you refuse to surrender, it's *believe or die* and you don't want to die, you make yourself the apostle of temperate climates and harvests generous as wedding feasts, prayers intoned without end, you bless the taste of bread and wine, the rituals that go on until nightfall, kisses proffered in secret to animal gods, prayers primitive because that's where you are from, what has given you the mettle to build arks for floods. You are pagan and intend to remain so.

Pagan, yes, you will remain. You were forced to translate so many epics in college that your brain is as peopled as Olympus. You belong to a vocabulary of legends and you still hear the grandeur of *polis* when it's *politics* you write, as if you could call down a bit of dignity from the heavens. Happily, you've learned to hold your pencil in your left hand. On the side of the heart, it's *believe or believe*, it's the blood of alliances and celebrations, even if they don't last forever. You've made your inventory of your arms, paper, pencils, nails, hammer, fingers, mouth, the ready tongue, the tongue that can revive dead ideas. You have not yet lost your memory.

Because your womb enjoins, your womb calls out, desire's tide, perspiration, wine of communion and intoxication. Once more you acknowledge your thirst, you shake shrouds out into table linen, you let no one scorn any longer the allure of light. Here is now, the mortification of being no one, here is everywhere, the same tears, the same arms, but love larger than fear. You still dare to raise up your pronoun, each morning you raise it up, a duteous task, an exercise kin to the conjugations your mother had you repeat every night after school. One day you stopped writing *I*, you forget why. Your memories had failed in their picturing.

Like an alcoholic's pledge, day after day the guerrilla war of living, teeming forests, the soul's strongholds to besiege. Hunkered down in your flesh, you spy out your smallest weaknesses, you permit yourself no quarter. For so long you've thought dark, seen dark, spoken dark in the blazing sun. Human nature is incurable, you've known that for a long time, you are legion in your solitude, this is no consolation, an observation at best. You have not done counting the empty chairs around you and you appraise them out of the corner of your eye, swearing you will not sit yourself there. It is upright that you want to inhabit yourself, upright among the living. You want to learn to say *us* as if you were summoning witnesses.

Notes

p. 30: The phrase in italics is from Charles Baudelaire.

p. 79: Phrases in italics are from Roland Giguère.

p. 93: The phrase in italics is from Anne Hébert.

About the Author

Born in Sherbrooke, Quebec, for over thirty years Louise Dupré has been one of the shining lights of that province's literary world. The author of some ten collections of poetry, as well as novels, stories, and essays, she has twice won the Grand Prix Québécor of the International Poetry Festival at Trois Rivières, and twice won the Governor General's Literary Award for French language poetry. Her work is characterized by austere lyricism and a profound reflection on the human condition. *La main hantée* was awarded the Governor General's Award for French language poetry in 2017.

About the Translator

Born in Winnipeg, Donald Winkler is a translator of fiction, non-fiction, and poetry. He is a three-time winner of the Governor General's Literary Award for French to English translation. He lives in Montreal.

Printed in November 2019
by Gauvin Press,
Gatineau, Québec